January 2020

May the call
Hear your Heart's
Desires.

Here is to your
Heart already
Answering
the Call!

Love much,
jospL

LAYING BARE THE BONES

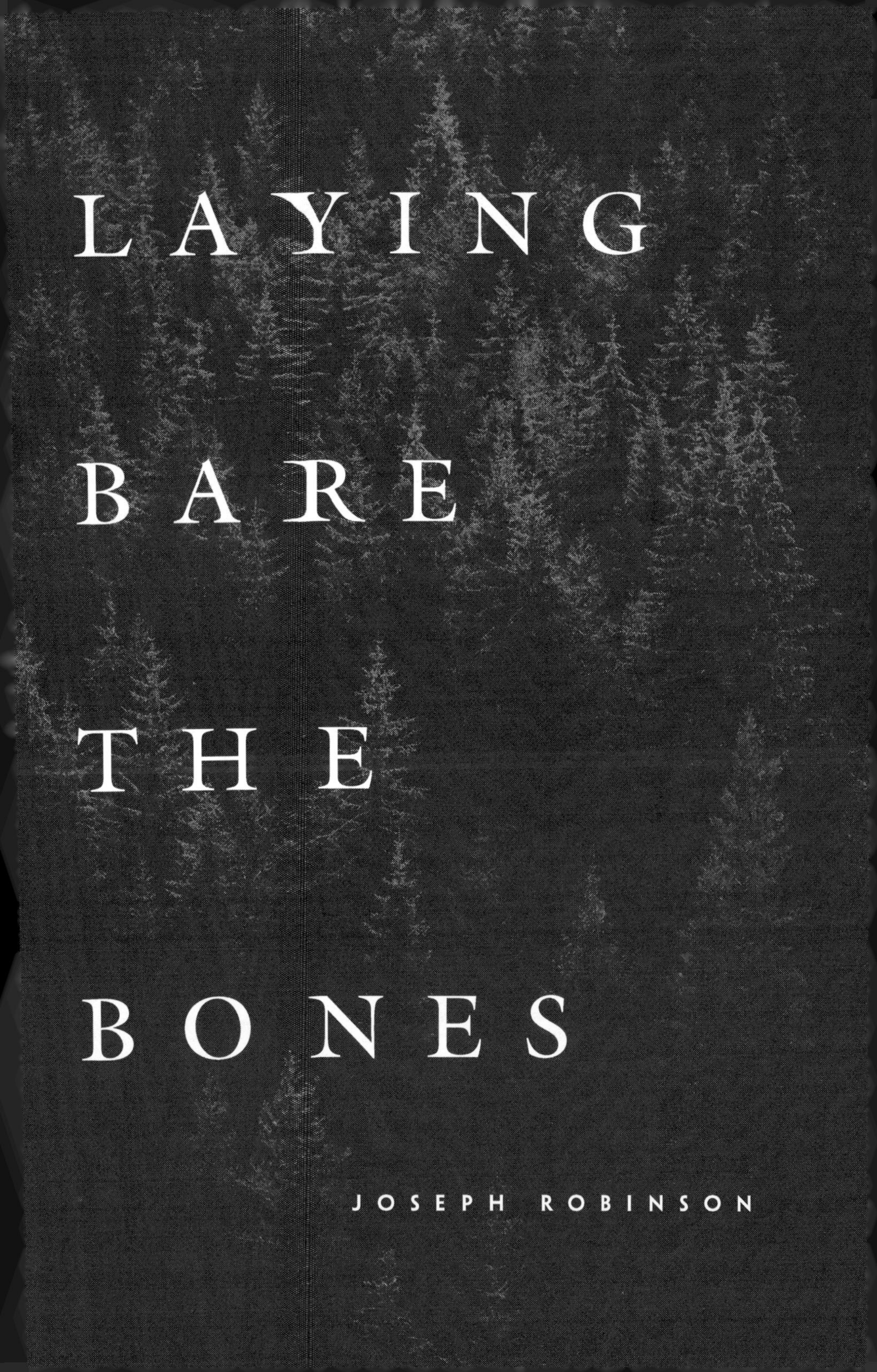

LAYING BARE THE BONES

JOSEPH ROBINSON

INSIDE OUT WISDOM
Newcastle, Washington

Look for soon-to-be–released works by Joseph Robinson:
Mystic Messenger, an eco-fable trilogy

More poetic musings, essays, and other
creative writing by Joseph Robinson:
www.insideoutwisdom.com

INSIDE OUT WISDOM
Newcastle, WA
ISBN: 978-1-7339903-0-1
Library of Congress Control Number:

Printed in the United States of America.
1st Edition 2019

Book Design by Kevin Barrett Kane
Edited by Joanna Dobson, ALTAI PILGRIM
Author photo by: Tove Danovich

Dedicated to Prema,
my muse and inspiration, always.

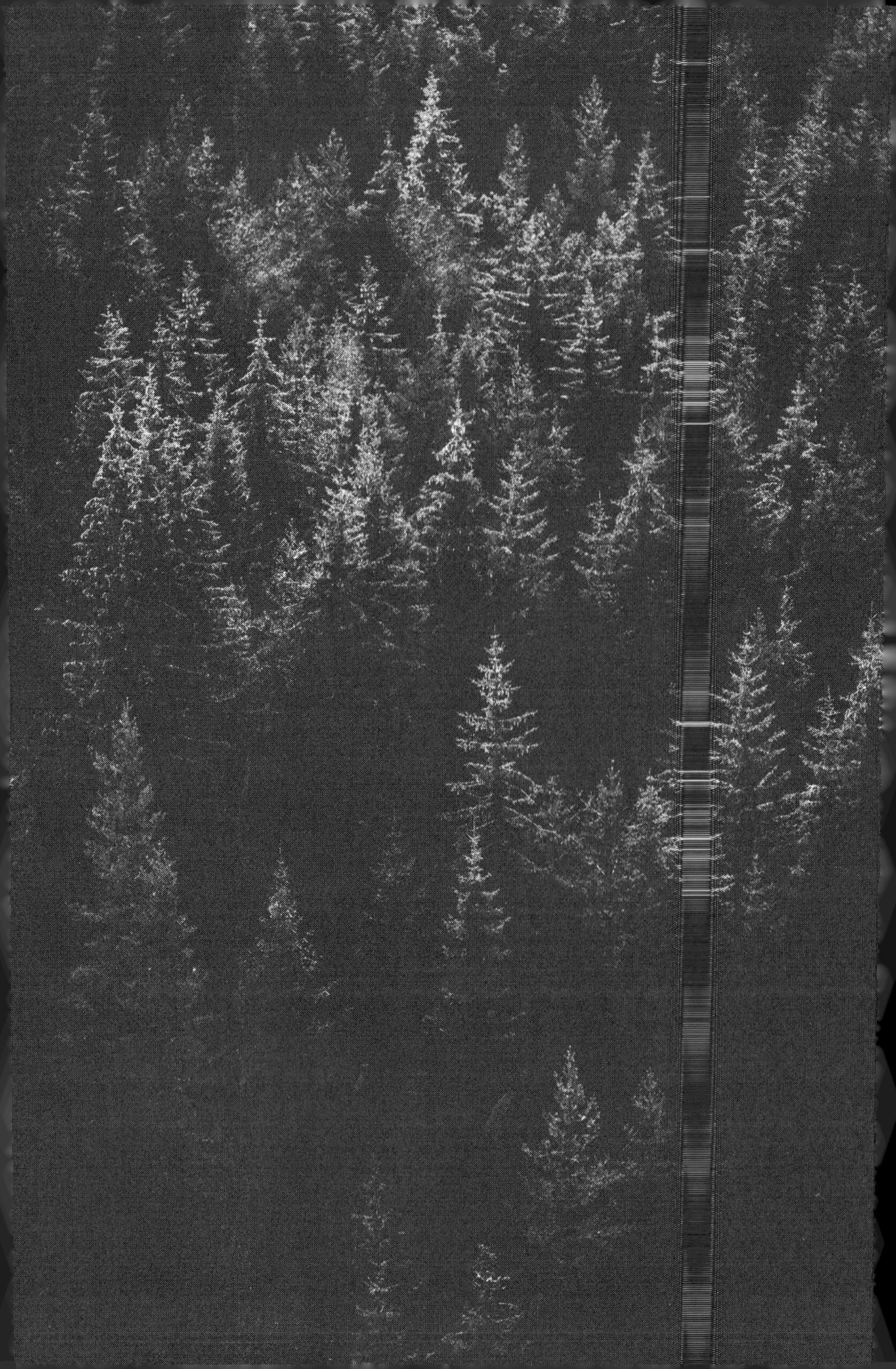

NOTE TO THE READER

You are the true explorer, the intrepid journeyer of the interior spaces and the deeper heart.

You, the storied soul, are pure inspiration to my inner voice and musings, as with yearning heart, I hope to awaken the healing of mind, body, and soul.

Evolution herself is calling you to open yet one more door, to bring with you community and conversation for the rest of us who are finding our way.

You make a difference opening the door of true compassion.

Welcome.

I

AWAITING THE CALL TO WALK UPON THE EARTH

We are lived by powers we pretend to understand.

— W. H. Auden

AWARENESS

We feel our way,
blind to the real world.

Fingers lightly flutter over
objects
here
&
there.

Ahh…
That's what I was looking for.

There.
No, not it.

Lost.
Found again.
Bliss.

BEGINNINGS

You begin by stepping out into the world.
You might just be hiding, hoping not to get wet in the rain.

There is an overhang on an old barn to shelter under until the storm passes.
As soon as the deluge stops, you consider your next step.

Feeling the way with outstretched arm, palm up.

Has it slowed enough?
Have the dark clouds passed?
You think to yourself,
what's a little rain going to hurt?

Then a part of you imagines the road,
now slippery and treacherous.
It is sure to ruin your shoes.

Reaching inside for courage,
putting one tenuous foot in front of the other,
tiptoeing through, knees high, sliding along the way,
You soak your socks.

Cold wet feet send forth a shiver of doubt:
Then, to hell with it.
Nothing can stop us now.

STRIVE

I wade into the world,
ignoring the puddles,
not caring what mother told me
about this or that.
Simple.
Divine.
Connected.

All of it just is
and that's ok.
Completeness made for you and me.
I truly don't know anything,
Yet,
I trust the depth of it — endless.

I seek forgiveness now,
for there are broken promises,
vows,
agreements.
Trust me
no more.
Fickle.

The heart,
however, true.
The nothing and the everything
have a voice.
One voice.
All hope echoes into the deep well of you,
where it shimmers back at me in the darkness and shadows.
The reflection of the moon,
clear as if really there.
Without you, it says,
I am nothing.

Who would hear this song?
Who would see the mountain?
What heart would feel the truth?

So, pride be silent.
Strive not my love,
of your own accord,
as I see you,
truly, I do,
And love you still.
Always.
Forever.

DEATH

The locomotive that came to pick up my Father   was of
the old kind:
Steel and iron riveted together by muscle and hammer.
It clanged, screeched, coughed steam and smoke,
belching acrid haze all over the place.
Scheduled to pick him up months (or more than a life-
time?) in advance — it raced.
Though it never really slowed, we hoped it would be late,
or
never come at all.
We knew, we'd miss him.
Miss him, deeply.
He was our hero, mentor, sage —
the Elder of our tribe:
strong and wise but weaker than we knew.
The cold wind blew.
The train bore down upon its destiny.
He bravely waited on the platform — not alone, but
singular.
He was the only passenger on this leg of the trip.
We worried, him waiting out there like that.
All dressed up in his best suit, along with that special tie
we picked out, he remembered:
wool: black like the night,

and to polish his shoes,
and put on new socks and underwear.
Nothing remained but to wait expectantly for a few days.
I heard the whistle from afar and walked out to the platform to say goodbye.
He was silent.
Waiting there with him, I shared my heart.
It was full of sorrow, fear, gratitude.
He had taught me much and was literally my reason for being.
That alone was worth being thankful for an eternity.
He gave me a slight nod in understanding and looked down the track at the coming calliope heading our way.
The waiting nearly drove me mad.
Frustrated and anxious, I paced.
He remained stoic and patient to the last.
Always just in time, the black mass stopped to pick him up promptly at 12:05,
just as he had arranged.
His wife and her sister, his daughter, and a daughter-in-law, along with his best friend
were there with me as the whole thing came to a stop.
We wept.
He ignored us, a slight smile across his face.
Peace awaited him in the dining car
where his Mother had prepared Apple Pie.
He could order anything he wanted to drink.
I thought, that must have pleased him.

I could see through the window as the locomotive began to leave, he was happy.
Chugging, railing, shaking, screaming its way forward and out of sight.
Many came later to say farewell
but it was too late.
He was gone
and
never coming back.
The truth is, I think he is happy.
His job well done, he gave it his best.
Satisfied: finally, he had figured it all out
although, he barely said a word about any of it
out there on the platform where we waited together.
He had secretly written it all down for us the year before, a masterpiece of gnosis, discovered back at home, tucked away in an old dresser drawer.
His Magnum Opus.
His truth.
Someday, the same train will come for me.
I hope I finish my work in time.
I started later than I should have.
Afraid as I was all these years.
The time with him, so brief, so profound,
gave me courage, gave me hope.
With his help, maybe I've figured it out just a bit more.
I now know, an ordinary map in an ordinary place can make a difference.

I remember, we used to skip stones down at the lake.
He would explain to me the cause and effect of waves
moving through time all the way across to the other
shore.
He told his tale,
walked to the station,
boarded the train,
all the while becoming a character to admire.
Maybe, I will be able to do the same.

INSPIRED

Heroes aren't born
they are inspired
by the call of duty
or the cry for help.

A place within stirs
to answer,
to bring protection,
to carry the fallen,
to extinguish the flame.

For when the alarms tone
they are ready,
prepared,
as best they can be.

With agency
and urgency,
they arrive,
heart in hand,
and when the work is done,
a de mob
and rehab begins.

Hotwash, as those around them
point out,
a hero
arose from within.
Humble in the face
of this,
they shrug off the accolades.

For those that know,
they recognize,
the real heroes
are those who answered the call
never to return
from their choice
to serve.

KIRTAN

The calliope warms emitting
pings and tings,
bumps and thumps
as a squelch barks out.

Welcome everyone to the stage.

God,
we are calling you,
unveiling your names,
asking for help.

Open my heart.
Free my soul.
Give me a voice.
It's been years and
nothing's changed.

Well, some things have.
A child raised in my lap
used to be near.
Loves have come and gone.
Now, it's only the faithful many
that I recognize as my kin.

They welcome me back.
It has been a long time.
The road is treacherous.
The journey full.
My heart bursts wide open.

Every night I sing.
My voice raw,
scarred over time.
It was God's ears
that consumed my song:
Krishna, Krishna,
Hari, Hari
More fire,
more shredding of me to you.

Vasudevaya.

Then a failing note still vainly clings
to the throat of the stricken one.
And we travel on
we singers of God.

Help us,
we need a chorus,
a response to our call.
Be here with me now
in my small humble arms,

wheezing and easing in harmony.

In,
then out,
the breath:
Samsara.
Thus, the ancient words
make notes
and pour out from soul to soul
for eternity.

REMEMBER

Perhaps I am like the Crocus in spring:
Too impatient to wait,
too stupid to know better.

I'm out of the running gate faster than I know.
The inspiration within,
compels me to push right away.

Then I'm alone in front, displaying all I have to give:
white, yellow, purple and green.

I'm bursting through the mud and snow and sleet,
enduring the cold.
Welcoming real warmth,
I'm happy when noticed.

Yes, it was an unplanned moment when you walked by
and spied me
from the corner of your eye.

Head hung low, thinking on your mind,
things to buy, people to please,
whole texts to finish all before time.

You were distracted for an instant.
Awakened by simply becoming aware.

We advanced creatures evolve,
to remind each other,
life is never as gloomy
as we think.

SELFISH

It's not all dreams and songs
and cabins in the woods.

The romance of the call to a blank page
is by a Siren or Muse all right,
albeit condemning
to a truly selfish act.

This, a destiny to crash upon the rocks.
broken then,
floating flotsam,
made stinky,
smelly,
of use
to no one.

Suddenly,
a small
clear
voice rises.

It took years just to learn how to listen for it.
Wait…

There it is again.
Gentle,
soft,
they whisper:
"just let go."

I am afraid,
of the life
I'd have sharing my voice
into the blank ethers of the Kosmos.

It's alright, they
beg of me:
We will catch you.

II

ACCEPTING THE JOURNEY INTO THE HEART OF THE WILD

They are to be admired those survivors of solitude
who have gone with no maps.

—John O'Donohue

SONG

No song today.

No loud burst of awareness
and that's ok.

Let me
alone
this way.

Talk not,
you mouth for story.

Sell me no more.

I'm only
interested in whispers —
the quiet ones,
and their nearly silent songs.

Their wealth is in
the rights of their totems,
their regalia,
their shared abundance.

As if a tiny lone
bird,
were bleeping and cheeping
their tune.

Wait.
Be still.
Listen.

Their heart calls for you
to save the only
life you can
save:
your own.

BELOVED

Adrift,
no course chartered except forward.

Turned by the wind.

Thrashed by the waves.

Wholly lost.

The infinite above,
the abyss below,
gratefully,
not alone.

Seeking refuge,
insights point a way towards solace.

Blessed be the calm course of this direction,
the horizon always promising.

Into her arms — an enduring embrace to behold -
an immense firmament of fluidity.
Grace, at last, inspires truth.

The ageless gives way to impermanence — ever growing,
flowing, emerging,
sharing her gifts without end.

That which is within and without cannot help but
express,
always open to embrace.

The seed rises to cloud the dawn,
obscuring the vastness,
providing a blanket of comfort
for the wounded soul.

Holding forever, to the bosom of beauty.

Drink this bounty deep.

Let it nourish the need
that masks the art of you.

Awaken now,
satiated in the moment by moment acceptance
of all that is.

Pull in closer, nuzzle next
to the timeless beat of life,
its ache enduring;
inviting to share the exchange.

One breath.

One love.

Eternal.

CONNECTIONS

In the predawn moment,
just before the light warms the morn,
a mist hangs over the ancient lake;
a stillness,
a quiet weighs upon the meadow.

All are in the dream.
The comings and goings,
the gatherings,
the chance crossings that cut deep across the marsh,
are yet to come on this day forward.

Pregnant potential swells the moment.
The 'all-of-it' wells up into a deep pause.
A breath pulled in.

Except for one —
a silent watcher,
with head sweeping slowly round,
as bright eyes ever sharp, keep vigil in the night, alone.

Downy feathers upon the wing
create a mask of awareness.

Evolution forms a face.
Deep listening as it takes it all in.

Hungry, it is all business.
Hooked beak,
talons.

A call,
inspired, announces itself from the shadows.

Who?
Who, indeed.
Who will join me in celebration of this day?

Who?
Who will dare to share in the light breaking,
light warming,
churning pure beauty for a chance glance from the
passer by?

In this world,
the deep well of the soul
is yearning with eternity,
expressed in an instant.

The 'all of it' waiting, waiting,
waiting for what's next.

A pang, an ache.
Yet, there is nothing to do.

Then, from across the way,
over the red brush and the moss,
and the little pillows of grass,
the brambles rattle and chatter in the breeze.

A cool wind,
sent as a last ditch effort,
fights off the inevitable
for just one moment more.

Anticipation and all,
sending a shiver
even through the brave.

A reminder of the wisdom,
or lack thereof,
in any given moment.

Who answers?
Who calls back?

Then it comes.

The sound returns
just in time,
to warm the heart of the watcher,
the witness,
and all who have just awakened.

EXISTENTIAL

The tree in my backyard is laughing at me
or
could it be the wind tickling its
underside, causing it to jiggle?

At times, it rises up fully,
arms extended,
in deep belly laughs.

Laughter lifts
the levity which
raised its chin and arms so high,
I even saw its pits.

Did I just see it cackle
to its feet?

Settling down into a mild chuckle
it shakes a bit
trying not to cry, I think.

Am I so funny as to
cause this ruckus?

What is it about my
simple stupidity
that causes
such commotion?

Aware enough,
at least,
to notice the trees
laughing at me.

Then,
I get the joke:
it's on me.
I forgot to laugh.

RECOGNITION

I barely recognize your face,
coming out of the mist.
Your features familiar yet foreign still.
How is it you can change so quickly?

Evolution left no time for me to say:
goodbye.

So, I am glad to see you once again.

Maybe the distance,
perhaps;
the longitude,
the latitude,
the places lost.

Bewildered.

It is with a tender touch
that I reach for your hand.
tentative,
yearning,
vulnerable in your presence.

My humbleness grows,
spying you in the reflection there,
just outside the periphery.
humbleness grows.

As the image of your face,
looks strangely like my own.

LIBERATION

I awoke to find you dancing with your firs,
swaying back and forth to the rhythm of the world,
pivoting in place while partnering with the wind,
the sound of which inspires me to sing.

An ode to nature, a tribute to you my darlings,
the ones I love: my mother, my lover, my bride;
daughter, sister, niece — creators all.

It is a marvel to see you dance,
calling me forth into the world,
daring me to join with your beauty.

I am shy at first,
feeling vulnerable
and clumsy.
paying no attention to my stumbling or my
awkwardness,
you beckon, inviting me to be free.

From deep inside
facing towards you,
the Truth

rises,
evolves,
wakes.

Showing my one Self,
contributing my small part,
breathless, I beg for a rest.
I must sit, must reflect.

Amazed, I ponder.
You, still dancing,
me, changed forever — liberated.

And all you did was move around the room, naked,
your firs flowing with the song of the breeze.

MORNING

There is a universe in my cup,
out of blackness, deep and dark.

The magical manifestation
swirls, spirals, and turns
as it infinitely expands
held firm there between my hands.

All I did was add a little cream:
and a whole cosmos revealed
itself to me.

I'm no god,
no saint,
nor sage,
a simple watcher and witness
to the unfolding of it all.

They come to me these creations,
happily entering into my
awareness
as I try to awaken.

Letting the roasted goodness
of the bitter beans
cool a bit
before I sip,
it occurs to me,
the hotness of a big bang
must be a lot like this.

One moment, calm nothingness,
and then
everything –
you,
me,
the dog,
and the next miracle.

Ahh..., pure joy arises.
Delight delivered on the rim,
the capacity at center,
tasting headless the
world before it.

Deliver me oh
happiness-in-my-hand
your clarity and warmth
to my heart.

For I need you this day and the next
to remind me
of my promise
to join the pattern,
after all,
from way out here
in wilds of pure potential.

Stimulate my memory,
sweet elixir,
that in every simple choice
whole worlds ascend
from my creation.

So, when I lay my head down at night
imaging the dawn,

it is you, conscious creator
who will greet me in kind.

Blessed be, the divine.

Whirling,
churning,
stirring,
there -
inside my mug.

UNKNOWN

The bird chirps in union
calling love home.

He's innocent of my listening.

He understands nothing
beyond my hearing.

Would he even exist
if there was no life here
to listen to his call?

There,
there:
a call back,
with its own voice, vaguely familiar —
yet utterly distinct.

He knows nothing
of stars,
and moons,
and suns,
and galaxies
far, far away.

No stories of old,
no hero's journey.
Just being alive
is journey enough.

His time: timeless.
His life: endless.

Breathing song:
completely unaware of years
and months
and the great churning
of the clockwork world.

Why is that reality lessor?

Surely being the happier one
might mean they are onto
something.

My little friend
knows only
peace
or fear.

Skirting from joy
to love
without

a care,

for he sees no cat
there in the tall grass or
the drama unfolding before my eyes.

And the cat
sees no car
cornering
too fast
and ignoring all the signs
that something is at play.

For if cat meets bird
and tire meets cat,
what of it?

It is said
in the great
halls of erudition
that this conversation
proves something.

My participation — all there is.
I don't really
know anything about all that.
Ignorant truly
of what is real.

For against the mass of it –
the sheer volume of life
itself,
is enough to give pause
to thinking.

Those hallowed halls
of gnosis crumble
away by detrition
without my help.

What use
are they
without peace?

For power?
For glory of God?
money....

In tasting those things
bitterness touches
my tongue with
biting bile.
Chase as they might,
I'm free,
somehow,
because of my not

knowing,
because I give up
to it all
— for the
the sake of all.

There is near silence now.

To confess, I secretly wanted to know,
and yet
finally tired of it, exhausted.

Gratitude washes through me.
Fear cannot abide within love.
Joy explodes from the great unknown.
Empty.

Beautiful nothing.

The bird,
the cat,
the car,
God,
and me
are
all annihilated.

III

JOINING NATURE'S SONG

"You've learned by now
to wait without waiting;

as if it were dusk
look into light falling:
in deep relief

things even out. Be
careless of nothing. See
what you see."

—Phillip Booth

BURNT TONGUE ON COFFEE

It was hot.

Said so,
right there on my cup:
"Careful, the beverage you're about to enjoy is extremely hot."

My tongue
stung.

My mind,
broke open.

My ego,
flew away.

Freed, like a long caged bird
so sure of itself
in its lone song.

Fly, fly away little bird.

What's this?
A golden thread
tied to its little leg.

A pure silken essence
showing me
where I hide:

Here you are.

Awe,
so small,
so sweet.

So,
beautiful.
I take you
in my hands.

You shit,
on my finger.

After wiping it off,
I kiss your tiny beak
and
give you a huge cage in which to sing.

Infinite,
absolute,
a marvel of a home.
no visible walls,
no thread,
nothing separated,
naught, nil, none.

I take another sip of coffee,
and burn my tongue again.

NATURE

Over miles and miles
of pounding pavement,
both literally and figuratively,
Nature eases
my suffering thoughts.

The wizened sage would say
we should not try to move
the hopeless mass to relief
as, just a tiny taste of freedom
is a cruel vision gifted in a light
that cannot be sustained.

Bullshit, I say
to the simpleton.

Appreciate you,
as I do,
but this is wrong.

Nature takes care of its own.

Sure, hours of nothingness,
sounds of the divine,

chants of gratitude,
prayers,
dances,
and beloved teachers —
all
have given selflessly to the mix.

Their genius
beguiles no one.

Better to leap headlong into the sea,
to which the very circumstance
offers the possibility of relief.
The desired communion with the beloved
does create the ultimate act of becoming.

The switch,
an accident?

Glorious surprise,
Nature was there all along.

With ancestors, kin, lovers,
the whole of creation awakening
to the moment revealing a reflective universe.
Pardon my enthusiasm for this ordinary thing,
but in the remembering

I am still awed
by this gift.

To the point, I do morn
the Guru -
lost.

We come to it.

Is relief even desired
if it is not permanent?

Don't forget the question
of forever.

Fleeting, ever moving,
flowing decay,
and effervescence.

Grateful am I to know,
the only thing granted permanence
is impermanence alone.

God, I see you there.

Pleased to thee, I sing.
How dare I act, then,
with reserve to protect,

either them
or me?

For in this realization
comes my freedom
to finally give up the illusion of control
and release into the arms
of the intelligence of All.

Back into the abyss,
bathing in it,
holding me as tight
as I hold it.

Always there for me in illusion
and Truth:
a part is a whole,
a slight glimpse enough
to set the connection — that brings
great fortune the facet to possess
a single instant of that which is.

NOT TWO

Many describe it as tumbling
down a deep hole.

Dark,
dank,
and full of the unknown.

I suppose it is right
to deploy the feeling of
g
r
a
v
i
t
y
at work,

a force beyond the control
of humble humans.

Massive,
mysterious,

miracle making
is its very nature.

Everything somehow affected
by its innocent being:
all that is.

We like thinking in the past.
How did it get here?
How does it work?
Why?
For how long?

For every answer,
another question
ad infinitum.

In that form,
it leaves me too cold
out there in deep space:
so far from home
with black holes sucking all
the light out of the room
by consuming whole stars
and galaxies and stuff.

Popcorn.

Just like when I eat popcorn.
Munch,
munch,
munch,
crunch.

Never really satisfied,
all the way down to the bottom
until the dead soldiers,
partially opened,
soaked in delicious salted butter,
become my last bit of perfect order
as I dab at the remains of the Kosmos,
finally breaking my attention
from all the drama played out
falsely before me.

Gone cold.
Not real.

It is all just one big illusion
chosen from a million choices all at once.

Home -
it is closer to home.

The source of 'ALL'
lives near me,

warm,
loving,

right next to me all the time,
like a friend remembered
for all the good times we had.

Ever distant now,
yet, utterly known.

True.

It was not always this way:
for being lost to love
is a big part of finding it.

A knowing grows as you gently,
harmoniously,
simply,
open to it
setting up residence within your tiny house.

There is no warning.
A little item of clothing left by mistake?
Maybe.

Then a satchel or kit filled with bits
here in the bathroom for convenience.

Fresh.
New.

There is life here
smelling ever so sweet.

Longer visits begin with timid response.
Whole suit-cases brought over
now filled with potential circumstance.

Dinner out,
a dance,
and then
a wedding or a funeral
where deep understanding
seduces you in a subtle slow show.

You are a couple now.

Two,
now: One.

Connected by unseen forces
stronger than any apple pulling Earth:
beyond space and time,
it is a power to be
reckoned with
but not in the usual way.

More ordinary.

So simple:
this being "not two."

Living life,
breathing in and out,
giving birth,
healing hurts,
growing old together.

We always travel with one another.

It really never was any other way.

I'd forgotten this Truth, then
remembered suddenly:

with my fingers in my mouth
fiddling, trying to pry out
a pesky husk from
between my teeth.

Ahh,
got it.
I spat it out unceremoniously from the
tip of my tongue:

Twtftht.

The yellow flaky kernel-bit
lands on the fuzzy little blanket covering my legs
blocking out the chill.

That's it.

The massive,
miraculous,
marvellous,
magnificent
grand,
glorious,
significant,
Kosmic,
evolutionary,
inspired,
joyous,
great center of the consciousness
of all
be-ing
of all
infinite,
absolute, aware creation
is
now inextricably
one.

God is,
and I Love.

EXPRESSING

Bending
towards the sun.

What hides there
brings me to my knees.

Knocked prone
by utter grandeur.

A colossal bloom,
delicate, crinkled, perfection.
Color,
texture,
aroma.

I'm in awe.

Your simplicity
is a masterpiece
of
expression.

You care less,
who sees you.

Possessing no self
you give your all to all your gifts.
It makes no difference that I bow in gratitude;
face full of tears at the sheer magnificence
of your very presence.

Nothing in you
judges me
even
if I were to rise from the shadows
and
stomp and stamp
you
back into the black earth.

But I won't.

Saved, I see my face in you.

Slightly aware, I am,
one with the God found reflected there.

I greet you.

Praying now to the root of all
realising my love

is in the petals
mirroring the absolute.

Is this perfection I see?

That which you share,
is never-ending,
and does not care I love you
as I do.

Yours is a free life
with never a thought of needful things.

Pain dare not dull
that which shines from your center.

My Beloved,
when did you
arrive?

Why are you hiding out back
between the weeds and brambles
of a forgotten fence line?

Thriving in the thorny thatch
of thicket run wild.
Pink and blood-red ribbons

of white and yellow
face forward toward
the warmth of morning.

Your light burns away the dew.

Suddenly, a lover buzzes by
rewarded by the essence.
You, burst in ecstasy
without ever knowing
another is even within your realm.

I beg of you
show
me how
to wither and die
in grace.

For in this place
we pass from fluorescence
to decay.

This brief
moment
in which we become
truly aware,
makes it worth

the effort
it takes all existence
to create.

INSIDE OUT

One might say that the place
with the shuttered windows and sealed doors
looks abandoned.

The gate locked,
the path to where guests are received
left to run wild.

Weeds,
leaves,
over grown shrubs
try to block the way.

All are gone.
Those that cared
what went on
left, by and by,
gladly moving to livelier locations.

You've seen those homes with windows aglow
in blue flickering shadows
as whole worlds play out endlessly within.
Wildness copied.

Freedom duplicated.
Hunger satisfied in mind.
Envy promoted to high art,
this medium,
fame and fortune,
and all that goes with it
— entertainment for the masses.

From inside,
the watcher remains silent.

Living fully without a care in the world.

Facing inward,
towards the Truth,
is all there really is.

Freedom comes,
knowing the clock hands don't really move forward,
because the light outside is no match
for that which emanates from within.

Bees have set up shop in the rafters of the porch:
their comings and goings real enough
to satisfy any wandering heart
with an eye for the horizon.

How could one not rejoice at knowing what's inside?

Dancing,
singing,
love making,
the kitchen busy as ever
turning that which has been gathered
into thick gobs of sweet nectar
in honor of the queen.

Move along passerby,
you who take no notice of the invitation to join
the only party of note.

Honest is the hum
heard in the heart
keeping beat with the song of the soul
attuned only there, within, where there is all that is
needed to sustain.

Inside is all that is needed to entertain everything to
which your loneliness calls.

Despite outward appearances,
Herein lies all that ever was.

Be still; listen, for the knower is aware.
Shy stirrings are heard
even when one tries to enter quietly,

perhaps through the side window,
hoping to sneak a little peek within.

Curiosity enlivens.

Then, we all burst out, SURPRISE!

Chairs are arranged quickly to make room for you at the head of the table.

You are invited to
sit,
eat,
dance,
love,
drink in,
no, gulp it in,
better yet,
swim within
our sweet honey of awe.

WHERE ALL THINGS END

I live
in a world of time
whereby, all things end.

Dread not,
this truth,
another awaits that we yet
again embrace.

Open both doors
of your heart.

One you use
to let the dog out.

The other you only open
when holding a garden party
and your friends
have all arrived.

Drinking, loving, eating, embracing;
all this,
when both are flung wide.
Don't believe the limit

of that which you can touch.

Fear no loss
when they all go home.

For the world within
expands as you
deny it all.

Sing, with that
which embraces you there.

Know,
let yourself be held.

Enter this conversation
with listening only,
as trifle utterances
accentuate your
separation.

How do you truly become one with everything?

Enter fully,
to that place which
lives
beyond the threshold;
out there

afar, infinitely broad.

Know,
the absolute is just
a small step through those doors
where nothing ends,
where love is all,
where all are loved.

THE LESSON

A question,
packed,
bundled with the rest of it to carry.

What path,
Beloved,
to take?

Towards a horizon,
over fields of yellow flowers,
over many mountains,
blue and green with hope.

A journey,
then,
over deep dark sea.

Heaving against the torrent tide,
wind
breaking open
the crests
revealing — white foam — frothing backward.

No easy answer it seems.

Having arrived,
welcomed by the spirits,
the round temple held my yearning soul.

I sighed.
"wake, dear one," Beloved called.

Dance with me.
Sing with me.
Love with me.

In every song the bird shrill;
soft pink and purple petals — vibrant;
honoured by the towering forest — ancient;
in tiny mushrooms on the fallen nurses;
to little beetles making their way across the expanse.

"I am here for you."
I
Am
Here
For
You.

In every face.
In every embrace.
In every heart

rescued from its prison.
Freed.

"Lay down your burden," Love said to me.
For you are the sower of seeds.

Spread them wherever you roam.

Be free of future destinations,
put down
the dreams
and live
into the one called:
now.

"Listen," Beloved whispered.
Follow the song
inside your heart.

IV

AWAKENING TO A DAWNING DAY

To live oneself means: to be one's own task. Never say that it is a pleasure to live oneself. It will be no joy but a long suffering since you must become your own creator.

—Carl Jung

FLOW

I've been working
all the livelong
day.

Started early,
left late
never ending —
how much you make?

Labor on
you
strong back –
how many miles of track?

Endless love,
over-time,
not tired,
never retired.

In the end,
my hands are numb,
hammer down,
I am done.

What'd you create,
Over all these days?
A life,
I'd say.

KNOWING

I know you as generous — giving unexpectedly,
unpredictable, you
saved me from drowning
in the cold dark sea.

Circling down,
spinning,
as I was,
with my own history,
my own brand of confusion.

You and I loved.

Many were the same
across much of the familiar
in all sense of the word.

How odd to contemplate the irony
of those intersections of time and space.

You tried to warn
when you thought it was
nearly time to leave.
Having invited you to feast

you regaled us with charm
ever gracious,
ever funny and most interesting.

I think we surprised each other,
our common inspirations,
at times exchanged,
with a knowing familiarity.

Allness, beingness, connectedness,
discussed freely and with ease.

We first met without you even knowing
who I really was —
your beloved companion leading you directly to me
from across the church yard.

I put down the historical artifact,
to give her a loving pet,
as you exclaimed, "she usually
isn't so friendly with strangers."

I didn't introduce my true self
that day.
It was a secret —
But she had known me for a couple of months by then
as a familiar smell in the other house and home.
You, non-the-wiser, either forgot or didn't

care when we met the following year
for our first unified feast day
and carved the meat we would share.

Having bent and folded
ourselves,
into new and marvellous
positions over time,
we shared hopes,
dreams,
and challenges.

I'm glad I was brave enough
that day to thank you before you left,
a stolen private moment
when I honoured you for your gifts.

Grateful, humble, and unassuming to the last,
you held my blessings
in return,
us, now friends, kindred spirits of a sort.

A friendship cut all too short
as things were just getting interesting.
The memory of you all that remains.

This our wink and bond, now blooms

into a final expression of love
at the end of it all.

I cannot help but carry you
forward
ever knowledgeable
our truths revealed.

Like the forest
that binds,
we are interconnected
and dependent
on each other
in the most
unexpected ways.

From root to shoot to crown,
the loamy Earth holds us
for such a brief time — aware.

Our supports bracing against
rock and wind,
as the wilds live
within and around us.

You and I,
our humanness, our story,
now preserved as part

of your history and legacy.

As being the kind one,
to a roaming minstrel
in a grave yard,
for all to see
under a tree.

THE GUEST

Late one evening, an unwelcome guest knocked on the door.

Arising from a fog around my chair, I stumbled to answer the unwanted call.
Confused and bewildered as they burst into my living room.

The guest began taking over the sofa, the desk, the tables and the chairs.
My kitchen was now ruled by the right food, the correct vitamins, the proper thing to drink.

What nerve!

The conversations always swung towards the un invited one. My friends and family can only talk about the guest, and what is going on between them and me.

At first, I humoured them.

Then, I tried to ignore the things they did.
And now, I'm sick of them and wish they would leave.
But, they won't.

Try as I might, I cannot ask the guest to go, waving
them out the door.
That would be bad manners,
my mother says.

I faced my guest and asked them what it was they
wanted me to know.

Nothing was answered.

Resting now, still, in my chair, my guest over there on
the sofa,
both of us silent
as we wait for the other to leave.

MORNING II

Doves balance on the line
over the green, gold grain
contemplating their love.

The mist and cloud kiss
the mountain surrounds,
and frame the terraced steps
that hold the fruit of life.

The air carries the call
of deeply moved creatures
across the realm.

Light edges upwards.

Rising to shine
in the clear blue expanse
silvery ribbons of soft shade shimmer
in the gentle breeze.

So what? The world asks.

This has been so
for all memory here.

It remains because
it has long been forgotten.

Stirred by longing to join
with the morn,
I awake deep in grief.

For no words could ever
bring this life to all.

And if All would come
to share, in this lost and hidden place,
then this Life
would no longer awaken as such.

COMPASSION

They tell me compassion can heal the world.

I don't know about healing
and only very little about this place.

The outside rushes by.

It is noisy.
It makes things.
It sells things.

I long for a place of peace.

Over there is ordinary,
and that's all right by me.

Maybe, inside of me is where compassion truly arises?

In the still woods,
where the snow has freshly fallen,
the whisper of the tiniest creature is enough
to call me out of my thoughts and listen to its voice.

"Can you hear me?"

POETIC

I showed bravery —
no, valour.

I stepped off the path
once, twice, and
yet again
my calendar did not fill.

My voice went unheard.

I stopped making the car payments.
I failed to join the conversation.

All of it repossessed.

I followed
the longing
into the unknown
spaces
seeking ground
where a meeting with the world
did not occur.

What is the silence
that met me there?

Why call if I am not heard,
have no reply?

No answer but the quiet
chirping from somewhere in the meadow.

Still.

Alone with myself,
I cried,
"Whatever shall I do?"

A cricket emerged
from the grass,
landing
on top of my foot.

I found its peace.

Truth given
by
the simplicity of a singular sound
made manifest by something other
than a throated call.

How had I gotten it all so wrong?

The cause is empty, nothing to say,
nothing to fix, nothing to become,
nothing to change,
no art, no harvest, no thing.

No story.

With that it leaped out into the wilds of the bramble
a final act of ordinary life.
A brief, mysterious existence
gone in an instant.

Glowing gratitude,
to my friend,
for showing me this place.

Hope abandoned,

I now live on — astounded.

MATINS

Life is a succession of awakenings
each and every morning.

The little birds
celebrate the coming of the day,
fully in song
they call,
respond,
sing Graces.

Toward the one they name
perfection, love, harmony, and beauty.
Aliveness
in all manner of form.

A conscious watcher
of nature and Truth.
That which you see
you've become.

Beloved.
One.
Creator extraordinaire.
Literally, a giver of life.

Family born.
Community made.
Whole generations sustained.

In the tapestry that is you,
a fine a weave as ever made.

Thread by thread to the end,
a flourish
of colour and yarn.

The scene woven,
through and through,
is spectacular.

I am forever grateful.
You truly see me and think enough of what is
there
to include me within.

Now, to sing your praises
like the chick-a-dees at morn.

To tell the tale of love
and why I'm truly here.

I call upon the nameless one at present
to help me share a humble perspective.

For I saw you that first time
and
it was love at first sight.

Yours a consciousness directly connected.
Born of joy.
Bringer of light.
The soulful teacher of the innocents.

You, express inspiration directly
every time we meet.

Every time I leave your presence,
I am,
left wanting
to know you even more,
to sit,
to dine,
to share
your insights, humor, and vision.

Your enthusiasm, I crave.
Like my teachers, from far away
I, giddily excited,
twitch to be at your side.

For you feed me,
cure me of my want and need.

You help me build a home.
You guide me to sustainment,
cheering me along the way!

All of me celebrates the day we met.
For I was welcomed into your family,
like no other.

I knew, right then,
this was the place for me.

Ever since, and especially now,
expressing your Truth without hesitation.

Recognising how brave you are,
bestowing kindness of heart
in the face of the darkest challenges,
for I am a little Trender true
and know the gift you've shared in light.

An honour you've bestowed upon everyone
and particularly felt by me.

In the olden days the name for you
would be Queen, Mother, or Wise Women.

The person we go to for inspiration of every kind.

For hope,
for enlightenment
for direction on the true path.

As in every age,
I yearn for this fine counsel.

And weep now
for the curse of our mortal form
with its propensity to separate in time,
space,
and distance
the embodied you who guides so aptly.

I grieve at
the thought
of losing your counsel.

Know, I love you,
honour you,
and pray for you.
These beatitudes given by the same intelligence
that brought us together.
These morning blessings I share with you
as a thanksgiving in kind.

For all you are,
for that which you've built,
to all those you've touched,
for all that you've shared.

I am enriched beyond expression
to know you.

LAYING BARE THE BONES

I stepped lightly, one early spring
during a walk
down an old logging road
near the brook.

Meandering down past the bend
avoiding lacy crystal mounds
of gleaming
rock candy
dotting the way ahead,
tipping through puddles of melt.

Cheeps and pecks and little flutters
guide the way.

The coming Spring on the horizon
occasionally brings warmth of future days
upon the shoulders of a Southern wind.
This, a day of hope, relieved us from the long chill.

Life is itching to get out and see,
to forage,
to scrape,
to uncover what has fallen,

to unblock that which has been iced over
in unmovable fortitude.

A gray brown mat of fur
lies across the path.

This great creature,
once bucked, snorted,
and ruled the herd
in this little corner of the universe,
here on Earth
in the home state
on the back 40
out along the line.

The tines and spikes on the gnarled head
give away its power and age,
a trophied magnificence.

Nothing but a gutless
fur bag of bones — now:
rattled,
scattered,
hither and yon
by God only knows
what picked him apart —
bared
with no meat left to share.

I tipped over the hide
with the corner of my wet
brown
boot.

Naked now.

With nothing left,
inside is outside
and outside is gone,
bleached,
white,
bloodless.

What says this existential find about death?

A coral of crows
declare it an illusion.

Enlightened one tell me,
is that really so?

Pain,
suffering,
the end of all ends
can be denied as easily as the truth be told.

Compassion in me
knows
better.
Experience unfolds in the face of everything.

The titmouse wants to know
peeking his little nose out from the eye hole in the skull.

Embodied by death
we live.

Jumping the corpse,
wonder seeks the reason.

Did the hunter
finally target you?

The irony of mortal wounds
won't give up its prize.

Or did God lay waste
to the victim?

The coldest winter — now nearly past —
had a killing frost,
the kind that inspires songs,

about the heartfelt yearning
of loves lost to the wilderness.

Starved then,
suffering,
servant of nature.

The act of giving up life
one bone at a time
gives pause:
broken-bodied,
flesh torn,
rotting away,
to the point of sheer ecstasy.

Pondering the chill,
the fading light beckons me home,
before I too become
annihilated by the darkness.

Turning around towards the setting sun,
Spirit whispers to me,
'the way to live an awakened life
is to let all
feed upon your heart'.

ACKNOWLEDGEMENTS AND APPRECIATIONS

Rarely does creative work take place in a vacuum and this anthology is no exception. It was not birthed by me alone. I have many others to thank for their contribution.

My parents, who are now passed away, for all the wanderlust they inspired in me. To my Sister Dana who was the first to share her poetic voice with me and show the way through her exploring and journeying on the path of awakening.

My life partner Prema, who has been a dedicated muse. Her Father Ron Keeshan and his sweet and generous wife Liz Keeshan made gifts that funded exploratory trips, cover design and consulting fees, and shared with me many a fine meal over which the progress of these pages was discussed.

To all my teachers from Robert Meyer in my High School English class who first gave me a love of poetic verse; Atum who invokes the Beloved on my behalf to dare to share my true one Self and the voice that accompanies the Truth. From Mexico, to Bhutan, to the "wilds" of Canada, Atum has been this work's true Spiritual Guide and wise mentor to its humble scribe.

To Joanna Dobson, whose expert and artistic editorial hand has kept many of these words from flying out of control and brought the thoughts found here, and the entire manuscript into something readable. Joanna, a true pilgrim, has been a loyal companion to this many-year endeavor. I could not have done it without her.

To designer Kevin Barret Kane for taking a 'self-published' work and shaping it into a professional one.

And to those dear souls who are the direct subjects of the songs inspired by their deaths: Ben, Syd, and Val.

ABOUT THE AUTHOR

Joseph Robinson lives in Newcastle, near Seattle Washington, USA. He shares a home with his partner and their beloved dog, Father Shamus, in the foothills of the Cascade Mountains of the West Coast of the North American Continent.

Joseph holds a degree in English and has traveled extensively; he's completed expeditions beginning in the Crocker Hills of his native Wisconsin, the back alleys of Chicago, then onto the vast continents of Asia, Europe, and the Arctic. He most recently traveled the Northwest Passage and the Southern Himalayan foothills of Bhutan. With plans to trek through Central Asia, the Amazon, and Siberia with groups sharing wisdom and experience through poetry and conversation. He expects to embark on pilgrimages to the Altai Mountains, Italy, and Northern Canada in the forthcoming years. Joseph is part of the community of the *Art of Spiritual Guidance*, as inspired by Atum O'Kane.

His life as a writer is stirred by a deep love of the world — Nature and the wild places, as well as the interior inspirations they point to. From there, in poems and tales, he draws maps of a ground both sacred and philosophical, in which he seeks reflection of the good, the beautiful and the true.